THE PARTY CULTURE THAT KILLS

A South African Guide With a Global Warning

by

Thuli Marutle Leigh

Copyright © 2025 by Thuli Marutle Leigh
All rights reserved.

No part of this book may be reproduced, stored in a retrieval system, or transmitted in any form or by any means—electronic, mechanical, photocopying, recording, or otherwise—without prior written permission from the author.

ISBN: 9781997482017
Cover Design: Thuli Marutle Leigh

This book is a work of nonfiction based on personal viewpoints, lived experiences, and social commentary. Names, details, and events may be adapted for clarity and privacy where necessary.

For permissions, collaborations, or enquiries:
mt.marutle@gmail.com

🥀 Dedication Page

For the daughters of this land.
The ones who were loved.
The ones who were misguided.
The ones who were failed.
The ones who survived.
And the ones who did not make it home.

May we learn to protect you,
to guide you,
to honor you,
and to raise you —
not bury you.

Preface

I did not write this book to judge anyone.
I wrote it because my heart is heavy.

More and more, we are seeing young women go out for a night of fun and never return home.
We see the missing posters.
We see the headlines.
We hear the crying.
And still — life goes on as if this is normal.

This is not about one story or one person.
It is about a pattern happening all around us — a culture that keeps repeating itself.

I grew up in a time when community was a village and parents were guardians.
Today, freedom is louder than caution, and image is louder than safety.

While this book was inspired by true stories and realities in South Africa, its message speaks to women and communities around the world.
The loss, the silence, the danger — they are not just South African problems.
They are human ones.

This is not a book of blame.
It is a mirror, a conversation, and a call to protect our daughters.

May it open our eyes, soften our hearts, and wake us up.

— Thuli Marutle Leigh

📃 Table of Contents

Part I — The Night That Changed Us
1. The Soft Life Dream
2. Alcohol, Image & Influence
3. Girls Who Don't Come Home

Part II — The Village That Went Silent
4. Where Were the Parents?
5. The Community That Stopped Watching
6. The Men in the Shadows

Part III — The Cost of Ignoring Pain
7. Danger in the Night: Streets, Rides & Rooms
8. Violence, Vulnerability & Silence

Part IV — Rebuilding Our Daughters' Safety
9. Homes That Teach and Protect
10. Sisterhood, Mentorship & Watchfulness
11. Bringing Back the Village

Part One

The Night That Changed Us

Chapter 1
The Soft Life Dream

There is a new language among our daughters — a language of luxury, ease, beauty and escape.
They call it "soft life."

The soft life is the dream of being unbothered.
No stress.
No struggle.
No pain.
Just enjoyment.

On social media, it looks like:
- Perfect nails
- Lashes and lace wigs
- Designer bags (real or not)
- Cocktails with glowing ice cubes
- Pretty pictures in lounges and hotel lobbies

It is not just an aesthetic — it is a statement:
"I deserve a life where nothing is hard."

But here is where generations begin to separate.

In our era, we were raised on a different gospel:

"Work hard now, so you can rest later."

We were told to:
- Wake up early
- Respect elders
- Save money
- Be disciplined
- Build slowly
- Earn the life we want

We understood the long road.
We understood waiting.

Today, many girls are being told:

"Life is short. Enjoy while you can."

And some of that is innocent — young people should enjoy their youth.
But there is another side:

The Soft Life Dream Has Become a Shortcut

Not because the girls are lazy —
but because the world around them has shifted.

South Africa is often ranked as having the second highest youth unemployment rate in the world (ages 15–24), frequently just behind Djibouti.

Even many who finish school do not find work.
Not because they didn't try — but because there are simply no jobs to get.

University is a luxury most families cannot afford.
A matric certificate is not enough to open doors.
There are talented, intelligent, hardworking daughters sitting at home with nothing to wake up for.

So the dream changes.

Hard work used to be a promise.
Now, for many, it feels like a lie that never paid off.

When a girl watches her mother work herself to the bone —
but still struggle with bills,
still sacrifice,
still carry stress in her shoulders —
what does "hard work pays off" look like?

To her, it looks like suffering without reward.

So she looks somewhere else for relief.

And the soft life becomes:
- A fantasy
- A performance
- A way to feel valuable in a world that makes her feel powerless

But to live a dream she cannot afford, she needs access:
- Access to men with money
- Access to tables in clubs
- Access to rides, rooms, weekends away
- Access to a lifestyle she did not earn, but needs to appear like she has

This dream did not come from laziness.
It came from lack:
- Lack of job opportunities
- Lack of financial support
- Lack of education access
- Lack of a system that creates fairness
- Lack of emotional affirmation
- Lack of being seen at home

When a girl cannot build her own life, she may begin to borrow one.

Borrow beauty.
Borrow luxury.
Borrow confidence.
Borrow belonging.
Borrow identity.

And wherever something must be borrowed —
there is always someone waiting to collect.

Men who know the cost.
Clubs that know the vulnerability.
A nightlife economy built on:
- Girls who want to be seen
- Girls who want to feel loved
- Girls who want to feel chosen
- Girls who were never given a chance to become who they could have been

The soft life dream did not break our daughters.
The world broke them first.

This chapter is not written to accuse or shame.
It is written to understand.

Because if we do not understand the longing,
we cannot confront the danger.

The girls are not chasing alcohol.
They are not chasing the club.
They are not even chasing attention.

They are chasing relief.
Relief from:
- Pressure
- Lack
- Hopelessness
- And the fear of being stuck in a life they did not choose

If we want to protect our daughters,
we must stop asking,
"Why are they like this?"

And start asking,

What has happened to them?

Because the soft life dream is not the problem.
The problem is the world that makes the dream feel necessary.

Chapter 2
Alcohol, Image & Influence

There is a reason alcohol appears in almost every picture of the "soft life."
Not because the drink is special — but because of what it represents.

A drink in the hand has become a symbol:
- Of confidence
- Of adulthood
- Of belonging
- Of being "that girl"
- Of being seen

For many young women, the drink is not the joy.
The image is.

The Image Economy

This is the first generation to live life on display.

Moments are no longer simply lived.
They are presented.

A night out isn't just:
- Good music
- Good company
- Good memories

Now it is:
- Content
- Aesthetic
- Proof that "I'm enjoying my life."

Where we, in our time, went out for the experience,
many girls today go out for the picture of the experience.

The club is not just a place to have fun —
it is a stage.

The lifestyle is curated through:
- Poses
- Angles
- Captions
- Lighting
- Who is watching

The goal is no longer to be happy —
but to look happy.

Alcohol as Confidence

Alcohol does not simply relax the body —
it quiets the mind.

The first drink loosens the shoulders.
The second softens the anxiety.
The third silences the overthinking.
The fourth erases the fear.

And the moment fear disappears,
danger becomes invisible.

Alcohol disconnects the instinct that once protected girls.
It blurs awareness.
It slows reaction.
It numbs caution.

Once upon a time, fear was a boundary.
Now alcohol removes the boundary.

The Competition to Look Happy

Girls are no longer comparing lives.
They are comparing images of lives.

And they are competing for:
- Likes
- Comments
- Views
- Follows

as if those numbers are income.
as if they measure beauty.
as if they prove success.

Meanwhile, many of the girls they admire online are:
- Pretending
- Performing
- Surviving
- Hiding pain behind filters

We are watching:
Happiness staged.
Pain edited.
Reality disguised.

Followers have become currency.
Validation has become oxygen.
Attention has become self-worth.

So the club becomes:
- The photoshoot
- The proof
- The stage

Instead of the moment.

Influence: Who Is Raising Our Girls?

There was a time when girls learned:
- How to carry themselves
- How to respect themselves
- How to move safely in the world

from mothers, aunties, big sisters, elder women, and community guidance.

Today, many girls are being raised by:
- Instagram Explore Pages
- TikTok trends
- Club promoters
- Influencers they don't know
- Other girls their age who are also lost

The performance of soft life has become a curriculum.

But no one is teaching:
- Self-worth
- Safety
- Discernment
- Boundaries
- How predators behave
- How danger hides in plain sight

They are only teaching:
- The pose
- The angle
- The caption
- The aesthetic
- The illusion

The Truth Beneath It All

The girls are not addicted to alcohol.
They are not addicted to clubs.
They are not addicted to nightlife.

They are addicted to feeling like they matter.

And in a world where:
- Love is inconsistent
- Money is scarce
- Opportunity is limited
- The future feels uncertain

the soft life becomes the only dream that feels reachable.

But the dream has sharp edges.

And the world waiting behind the bottle does not love them.

Where This Leads

This is why so many heartbreaking stories begin the same way:

"She went out. She was laughing. She posted. She was seen alive. And then…"

Chapter 3
Girls Who don't come home

It always starts the same way.

Someone is doing makeup.
Someone is taking mirror pictures.
Someone is laughing in the background.
Someone is calling an Uber.
Someone is shouting, "Hurry up! We're late!"

There is music playing.
Perfume in the air.
Heels on the floor.
Phones charging for the pictures that must be taken.

The group leaves the house glowing.
Soft life activated.
Energy high.
Nothing heavy.
Nothing deep.

Just vibes.

And for a while — it is fun.

The music is good.
The lights are beautiful.

Everyone looks like they're living.
The night feels easy.
She feels pretty.
She feels chosen.
She feels alive.

But nights don't stay still.

Nights move.

The Shift

There is always a moment — small and quiet — where the energy changes.

Maybe someone is too drunk.
Maybe someone disappeared with a guy.
Maybe someone got separated from the group.
Maybe someone lost her phone.
Maybe someone is now dancing with strangers.
Maybe someone is outside.
Maybe someone is sitting alone.
Maybe someone is trusting a ride offered by someone she barely knows.

No screaming.
No chaos.
No warning.

Just a shift.

A small, quiet, soft shift —

that no one notices until the sun comes up.

The Walk to Nowhere

It might look like:

- A quick ride home.
- A stop at another location.
- A "We're just going to chill."
- A detour.
- A promise of safety.
- A smile that looks harmless.
- A voice that sounds gentle.

Danger does not look like danger.
It looks familiar.

It looks friendly.
It looks harmless.
It looks like, "Don't worry, I got you."

Until it doesn't.

———

The Silence of the Morning

The next day is when the story changes.

One friend wakes up and checks her phone.
No message.
No "I'm home."
No blue ticks.
No replies.

At first, it's confusion.

Then:
- Calls.
- Texts.
- Voice notes.
- "Anyone heard from her?"
- "Check her location."
- "Try her mother."
- "Please phone again."
- "Maybe she slept at someone's place."

Then the stomach drops.

Because there is a kind of silence that is not just silence.

It is warning.

The Timeline Response

By afternoon:
- Someone posts her picture in a group chat.
- Someone asks in a WhatsApp status.
- Someone says, "Anyone seen her?"
- Someone tweets her name.

The comments come:
- "Yoh, hope she's okay."
- "She was out last night."
- "I saw her at the club."
- "What happened?"

But people scroll.
Because we have seen this before.

Too many times.

The Reality That Hurts to Say

Not every girl who goes out comes home.

Some are found.
Some are not.
Some return, but they are not the same after.

And some come home in ways no family should ever experience.

This chapter is not about fear.
It is about truth.

The world outside is not soft.
The night is not gentle.
The streets are not safe for young women.

And the saddest part?

Many of our girls do not know that.

No one told them:

- What danger looks like before it becomes danger.
- How predators study the drunkest girl in the room.
- How men use alcohol as invitation, not generosity.
- How girls get separated, not stolen.
- How safety requires strategy, not assumptions.

They were taught:
"Enjoy your youth."
But not:
"Come home alive."

Not Every Story Makes Headlines

Most tragedies are quiet.

A family crying behind closed doors.
A mother staring at a phone in disbelief.
A father pacing outside.
A sibling asking, "Where is she?"
A cousin printing posters.
A friend replaying the night in her mind, blaming herself.

The world goes on.
Life continues.
Until the next girl goes missing.

And the story repeats.

This Is Where We Must Wake Up

Girls are not disappearing because they are reckless.
They are disappearing because the world is dangerous
and the culture is lying to them.

The soft life dream does not show:

- The risks of separation
- The dangers of alcohol
- The intentions of some men
- The reality of the night
- The predators who watch quietly

Instagram does not show the end of the story.
Only the beginning.

PART TWO

The Village That Went Silent

Chapter 4
Where Were The Parents?

Whenever a tragedy happens, the first question people ask is:
"Where were the parents?"

It is an easy question.
A heavy one.
And often — an unfair one.

There are parents who raised their daughters with:
- Love
- Rules
- Boundaries
- Discipline
- Conversations
- Warnings
- Protection

There are parents who showed the way, who were present, who tried, who prayed, who guided.

And still…
Some children stray.

Not because the parents failed.
But because life outside the home has more voices than the home does.

The Shift Happens Slowly

Many girls are raised well — truly raised.
They know right from wrong.
They know danger.
They know the values of home.

But when they:
- Leave for university
- Move to res
- Start working
- Or simply gain freedom

the world opens up in a new way.

This is often the first time:
- No one checks what time they return
- No one asks who they are with
- No one says, "Come home"
- No one protects them from themselves

Not because the parents failed.
But because life outside the home has more voices than the home does.

The Shift Happens Slowly

Many girls are raised well — truly raised.
They know right from wrong.
They know danger.
They know the values of home.

But when they:
- Leave for university
- Move to res
- Start working
- Or simply gain freedom

the world opens up in a new way.

This is often the first time:
- No one checks what time they return
- No one asks who they are with
- No one says, "Come home"
- No one protects them from themselves

And freedom without structure becomes a classroom of its own.

Some learn quickly.
Some learn slowly.
Some learn painfully.

When Guidance Meets Choice

There is a saying in my language:

"Moipolai ga llelwe."
"One who destroys themselves cannot expect mourning."

But we must apply this carefully.

It does not mean:
• We do not love our children
• We do not feel pain when they make harmful choices
• We do not care what happens to them

The proverb means:

A parent can guide — but a child must choose.
And every choice has a consequence.

What the proverb teaches is:
- You can be taught the difference between fire and safety
- But if you walk into fire knowingly, the burn is not surprising

It speaks to accountability, not blame.

It reminds us that:

Guidance is offered — but responsibility is personal.

And this is where parenting ends and adulthood begins.

The Pain No Parent Says Out Loud

There are parents who lie awake at night thinking:
- "Where did I go wrong?"
- "What didn't I teach?"
- "Why didn't she listen?"
- "Was I too strict?"
- "Was I too soft?"

But sometimes…
There is no answer.

Sometimes the child did know better —
but the world felt louder than your voice.

And that is not failure.
That is life.

But We Must Also Tell the Other Truth

There are also households where parenting is minimal or missing.

Parents who:
- Set no curfews
- Ask no questions
- Do not know their children's friends
- Do not check where their daughters sleep
- Do not ask who pays for the outings
- Avoid confrontation and call it "giving freedom"

There is a difference between:
- Love, and
- Letting a child raise themselves

Some parents are exhausted — physically, financially, emotionally.
Some are hurt people raising hurt children.
Some were never parented themselves and are learning by trial and error.
Some are doing the best they can with very little support.

We do not judge them.
But we must acknowledge that:
Love alone is not guidance.
Providing is not parenting.
Silence is not wisdom.
Absence is not freedom.

A child without structure will seek structure somewhere else.
And the world outside is not gentle.

The Village That Faded

Once, the community helped raise children.
If a girl was seen where she should not be,
the whole neighborhood corrected her.

Now, people say:

"She's not my child."
"It's not my business."
"Let her live her life."

We lost something when we lost collective guidance.

A child raised by the internet is raised by strangers.
A child raised by social media is raised by performance.
A child raised without watchfulness must learn the world by impact.

We Must Hold Space for Two Truths

Truth 1:
There are parents who were present, loving, guiding, protective —
and their children still walked into danger.

Truth 2:
There are parents who were absent —
emotionally, physically, or both —
and their children had to raise themselves in a world that does not love them.

These truths can exist together.
No finger needs to be pointed.

Because the purpose of this conversation is not to blame,
but to understand where the safety tore open.

What We Must Remember

No girl deserves harm.
No daughter deserves to disappear.
No child deserves danger.

Victims are never responsible for what others choose to do to them.

Our conversation is not about blaming girls for going out.
It is about rebuilding the safety net underneath them.

We are not saying:
"Don't go out."

We are saying:
"Know how to come home."

We are not saying:
"Fear the world."

We are saying:
"Understand the world."

Because love without guidance is not love. Freedom without boundaries is not safety.

And a village that is silent cannot protect its daughters.

Chapter 5
The Community That Stopped Watching

Once, a child did not belong to one household.
A child belonged to the village.

If you were seen somewhere you shouldn't be,
your mother knew before you even got home —
not because of gossip,
but because someone cared enough to speak up.

A generation ago, we were raised by:
- Aunties who watched from the gate,
- Uncles who noticed everything,
- Neighbours who were like extended parents,
- Elders whose presence alone corrected us.

We respected every adult.
We feared disappointing any elder — not just our biological parents.

Because every elder was our parent.
Every older woman was "Mama."
Every older man was "Papa" or "Malome."
Every grandmother was "Koko."
Every grandfather was "Rakgolo."

There was no such thing as "That's not my child."

Every child was our child.

How the Village Protected Us

If a neighbour saw you with a boy —
whether young or old —
she didn't just watch silently.

She walked straight toward you.

She would say:

"O dira eng moo?"
What are you doing here?

And the boy would leave. In most cases a girl would even run home before the neighbour even got close.

No argument.
No attitude.
Respect.

If a neighbour saw you getting into a car,
she didn't turn away.

She took the number plate.
She memorized the registration.
She reported it to your mother.

Not to embarrass you.
Not to shame you.
To protect your life.

If an elder told you to go home,
you went home.

Immediately.

Not because they were controlling —
but because we trusted their wisdom.
We knew they loved us, even in correction.

The Village Was Our Safety Net

Our community was not perfect.
But it was present.

It was watchful.
It was alert.
It was connected.

We grew up knowing:

"O bona motho mogolo, otshabe."
When you see an elder, straighten yourself.

We did not fear punishment.
We feared disappointing the people who raised us.

There was honor in respect.
There was safety in discipline.
There was protection in being seen.

The streets were not safe —
but the villagers were.

Our daughters today walk into the same streets —
but without the village behind them.

How the Village Disappeared

This loss didn't happen overnight.

1. Pride & Defensiveness Grew

Correcting a child now leads to:
- "Don't tell my child what to do"/"ungenaphi"
- "You think you're better than us."
- "Focus on your own life."

The moment correction became insult,
the village retreated.

2. Everyone Minds Their Own Business

We call it "privacy."
But it is really isolation.

Families became islands.
And islands drown alone.

3. Pain Made People Silent

Many adults today are wounded.
Exhausted.
Barely holding themselves together.

It's hard to protect others when you are in survival mode.

4. Social Media Replaced Community

But online attention does not protect them in real danger.

The village protected the body.
Social media only protects the image.

The Cost of Losing the Village

When the village stops watching,
the child walks alone,
even in a crowd.

No one says:
- "This place is not safe."
- "That man is too old for you."
- "Come home."
- "I saw something wrong."

And by the time we speak —
it is during the funeral speeches.

We are crying over tragedies
we could have prevented
if only we had spoken one week earlier.

Rebuilding the Village

We are not too late.

The village is not dead.
It is sleeping.

We need to wake it gently but firmly.

1. Speak Up Again

If you see danger — speak.
With love.
Without shame.

2. Correct Without Shaming

Guidance protects.
Judgment destroys.
Choose guidance.

3. Reconnect Women Across Generations

Big sisters mentor little sisters.
Aunties guide.
Mothers teach.
No girl should navigate the world alone.

4. Bring Good Men Into Protection

Fathers.
Brothers.
Uncles.
Men of integrity.

Male protection is not control.
It is safety.

5. Normalize Checking In

"Where are you?"
"How are you getting home?"
"Who are you with?"
"Are you okay?"

Not to monitor.
But to protect.

We Return to "My Child Is Our Child"

If we want our daughters to come home,
we must return to:
- Shared wisdom
- Shared responsibility
- Shared watchfulness
- Shared love

Because a girl raised by a village walks with an army behind her.

And an army comes home.

Chapter 6
The Men In The Shadows

Not every man is a danger.
Not every man intends harm.
There are men who protect, care, guide, and love with dignity.

But there is another kind of man,
and it is this kind we must speak about:

The man who watches.

He does not chase.
He observes.
He looks for the girl who needs attention,
validation, escape, or admiration.
He waits for opportunity, not connection.

Predators Don't Arrive Looking Like Threats

They do not come with warnings.
They come with:
- Charm
- Confidence
- Attention
- Generosity

They offer drinks, compliments, and comfort.

Danger does not begin with violence.
It begins with a gift.

The "Free Drink" Is Not Free

We need to say this clearly:

Some men use alcohol as currency.
They are not buying drinks — they are buying access.

A girl may think:

"It's just a drink."

But he may think:

"I bought access."

And access, in his mind, means:
- Her time
- Her body
- Her obedience
- Her silence

Because the drink was never kindness.
It was a contract she didn't know she was signing.

This is why:
A girl must never go out depending on men to fund the night.

If you cannot afford the night:
- The drinks
- The Uber home
- The entry fees
- The emergency backup

Then the night is already a risk.

Your money is your protection.

Without it, someone else has power.
And power in the wrong hands becomes danger.

The Flashy Car Fantasy

Many girls are drawn to:
- Flashy cars
- Designer clothes
- Men who look like "soft life providers"

But we must ask:
Why admire the man instead of admiring the lifestyle itself — and working towards it yourself?

We must teach our daughters:

Don't chase the man with the car.
Work until you can buy the car yourself.

Not to compete.
Not to impress.
But to be free.

Because when you depend on a man for luxury, your safety is in his hands.

But when you earn your own, your safety is in yours.

When the Friend Becomes the Bridge to Danger

This is a reality many don't want to speak about:

Sometimes danger does not come from a stranger.
Sometimes it comes through a friend.

A friend who says:
- "Let's go to that table."
- "They're buying drinks for us."
- "He said he'll take care of us."
- "Just relax, they're nice guys."

But sometimes:
- She wants to be liked.
- She wants to look connected.
- She wants to be seen.
- She wants her own night funded.

And without intending to,
she offers her friend as part of the exchange.

Not always out of malice.
Sometimes out of emptiness.
Sometimes out of pressure.
Sometimes because she, too, is trying to survive the moment.

But the result is the same:

The table was never just a table.
It was an entry point.

The "connection" was never just a social moment.
It was a setup, even if unintentional.

And friendships have ended in those moments.
Lives have changed in those moments.
Girls have disappeared in those moments.

What Protection Looks Like Now

We do not teach girls to fear men.
We teach them to read intention and prepare themselves.

We teach them:
- Have your own money.
- Have your own ride home planned.
- Keep your phone charged.
- Move in groups and leave together.
- Know your limits with alcohol.
- Do not go where you do not have power. Also be of age, your parents are the ones to decide if they think you are old enough to go out especially in the night and what measures will they put in place to ensure safety.

And we teach them:

Safety is not luck.
Safety is strategy.

A Father's Protection Is Not Control — It Is Love

My father drove me to parties.
He fetched fetched me again.
He made sure I had my own money.
Enough to enjoy, not enough to lose myself.
He was always reachable — always ready and on speed dial in case I decided he should fetch me sooner than we agreed.
Also I was already of age and he made sure I don't make partying a hobby and concentrated on important things like school.

That was not strictness.
That was structure.
That was love in action.

The goal is not to stop girls from going out.
The goal is to make sure they come home.

PART THREE
The Cost Of Ignoring Pain

Chapter 7

Danger In The Night: Streets, Rides & Rooms

The most dangerous part of the night is not always the club.
It is everything that happens after.

The street when the music ends.
The walk to the car.
The drive home.
The "after-party."
The room you were not planning to enter.

Danger does not arrive with alarms.
It arrives in the quiet moments.

The Street After the Party

Outside, the energy changes:
- People are drunk
- People are emotional
- People are unpredictable

And awareness is low.

Girls are tired.
Heels are painful.

Phones are dying.
Voices are slurred.
Friends get separated.

Predators do not attack when the music is loud.
They wait until girls are unguarded.

The Ride Home Is Not Automatically Safety

There was a time when getting into a car meant:

"I am almost home."

But today, we have seen situations where:
- A driver takes "a different route"
- A driver "forgets" to lock or unlock the doors
- The car stops in an isolated place
- Someone else joins the vehicle unexpectedly
- The driver pretends the car is "having a problem" to pull over
- The ride becomes a setup instead of a journey

Not all drivers are dangerous.
But you do not know which one is which.

That is why:

Your safety must never depend on a stranger.

If you cannot:
- Pay for your own ride
- Track your own journey
- Call someone instantly
- Get out if your instincts warn you

You are not safe.

Plan the Way Home Before You Leave the House

Safety is not something you figure out at 2AM. Safety is planned at 8PM while you are getting ready.

Ask:
1. Who is our sober driver?
2. Who is responsible for getting everyone home?
3. Who is keeping their phone charged?
4. Do we have emergency money?
5. If plans change, who do we call?

If none of these questions can be answered:

The night is unsafe before it even begins.

It is not controlling to plan.
It is survival.

If There Is No Safe Way Home — Don't Go

Let's say this clearly:

If you cannot fund your own fun, you are not ready for that fun.

If:
- You cannot pay your own transport
- You cannot buy your own beverages
- You cannot leave when you want to
- You depend on someone else to make the night possible

Then you have no protection.

Freedom without safety is not freedom.
It is exposure.

Limit the Alcohol

Alcohol is where awareness ends.
Once awareness ends, safety ends.

Know your limit.
Do not compete.
Do not drink what you cannot handle.
Do not black out in public.
Do not hand your mind to strangers.

Your body deserves better.
Your life deserves better.
You deserve better.

Move Together. Leave Together. Come Home Together.

If you arrived as five girls,
you go home as five girls.

No one gets left.
No one disappears.
No one leaves alone.
No one is "fine."
No one is "handling it."

This is sisterhood.
This is protection.
This is survival.

Your Life Is Worth More Than a Night Out

One night of fun is not worth:
- Your safety
- Your future
- Your body
- Your peace
- Your family's heartbreak

Choose life, every single time.

Chapter 8
Violence, Vulnerable & Silence

No girl goes out expecting danger.
No girl plans to disappear.
No girl anticipates harm.

Most girls leave home saying:

"I'll be back."

But the world has become a place where a girl
can be laughing at 10PM
and missing at 6AM.

This chapter is not written to create fear —
but to awaken awareness.

Because safety is not paranoia.
Safety is wisdom.

How Vulnerability Happens

Violence does not always begin with violence.
It begins with:
- Trust
- Comfort
- Alcohol
- Distraction
- Assumptions

A girl does not become vulnerable because she is careless.
She becomes vulnerable because she believes she is safe in that moment.

And belief can be dangerous.

Not All Men Who Become Dangerous Are "Hunters"

Some men do plan,
watching for the girl who is:
- Drunk
- Emotional
- Alone
- Unprotected

These men look for vulnerability.

But there is another group of men we must talk about:

Men who do not intend harm —
but become dangerous when drunk.

Men who:
- Cannot control their anger when intoxicated
- Become aggressive when they feel "rejected"
- Feel entitled when they have paid for drinks
- Lose empathy under the influence
- Turn violent when their pride is bruised

Alcohol does not create their character —
it reveals it.
And magnifies it.

A sober man who is respectful
may be safe.

But a drunk man with ego and no self-control
is a risk.

This is why we say:

Do not only watch how a man behaves when he is kind.
Watch how he behaves when he is drunk, frustrated, disappointed, or told "no."

That is where his truth lives.

Alcohol Has Consequences — For Everyone

This is why girls must learn:
- Do not abuse alcohol.
- Do not get so drunk that your mind can't protect your body.
- Do not ignore a friend who is drinking too much.
- Do not stay in relationships with people who drink recklessly.
- Do not party with someone who becomes a different person when drunk.

If alcohol changes a person into someone you would not trust — leave.

Because nothing good grows where:
- Alcohol is uncontrolled
- Anger is uncontrolled
- Ego is uncontrolled

A person who has no control over their drinking cannot protect you.
And often, cannot protect themselves.

Silence Protects Predators — and Violence Fueled by Intoxication

Girls are often taught to:
- "Keep the peace"
- "Don't embarrass him"
- "Don't speak up"
- "Don't make things awkward"

And so they stay in situations their bodies are screaming about.

We must teach:

If something feels wrong, leave immediately. Your safety is more important than someone else's feelings.

A girl who uses her voice is harder to harm.

A girl who ignores her instincts walks alone.

Pain That Is Not Spoken Turns Into Silence That Kills

Violence is not only physical.
Harm can also be:
- Emotional
- Psychological
- Sexual
- Spiritual

A girl can come home smiling
but carry a silent wound.

So we do not shame her for what happened.
We make space for her to speak.
We believe her.
We walk with her through healing, not judgment.

Because blame does not save lives.
Awareness does.
Wisdom does.
Community does.

Vulnerability Is Not Weakness — It Is Humanity

Girls want:
- To be loved
- To feel beautiful
- To be seen
- To feel chosen

These desires are not foolish.
They are human.

The answer is not to teach girls to stop wanting love, belonging, beauty, attention or joy.
The answer is to teach them how to protect themselves while wanting these things.

To teach them:
- How to choose friends wisely
- How to recognize predatory behavior
- How to read a man's character beyond charm
- How to trust instincts
- How to stay aware and safe
- How to leave when something feels wrong

Because the desire to be loved is not the danger.
The danger is seeking love in unsafe places.

PART FOUR
Rebuilding Our Daughters Safety

Chapter 9
Homes That Teach & Protect

Safety begins long before a girl enters the world.
It begins at home — not in fear, but in conversation, structure, and active love.

A strong home does not remove all danger,
but it gives a girl:

- A compass
- A voice
- A standard
- A sense of self
- And a place to return to

That is what saves lives.

Love Is Not Enough — Direction Is Needed

Many parents love their children.
But love that is silent is not enough.
Love must be expressed as guidance.

A child needs to be taught:

- Self-worth
- Instinct
- Responsibility
- Discernment
- Boundaries
- Awareness

Love that does not prepare is not protection.
Love that does not guide is not safety.

The Power of Integrity

We must teach our children, especially daughters, about integrity —
doing the right thing even when no one is watching,
even when no one will find out,
even when your parents live far away.

Integrity is what keeps you safe when supervision ends.

Tell them:

"Integrity is who you are when no one is around to remind you."

Teach them that:

- It is not every weekend that one must be out.
- The night will still exist tomorrow.
- Not all fun is worth the risk.

True maturity is learning when to say:

"I'll stay home tonight."

Because sometimes peace is better than nightlife.

The Place of Alcohol — Awareness, Not Denial

Alcohol has become part of modern youth culture,
but we must teach its boundaries.

Teach children and young adults that:

- Alcohol is not what makes life exciting.
- It is not a symbol of adulthood.
- It is not confidence in a bottle.
- It is not escape from pain.

It is meant for occasional enjoyment — not daily habit.
It is for celebration, not dependence.
And there must always be a limit.

Ask them:

"Why did you decide to drink?"
"Is it joy or pressure?"
"Is it choice or imitation?"

When drinking becomes identity,
danger follows —
because decision-making disappears where alcohol controls the mind.

Remind them:

"If you cannot drink responsibly, do not drink at all."
"If you cannot stop once you start, you are not in control."

And if they are surrounded by people who abuse alcohol —
friends, partners, or peers —
teach them to walk away.
Because nothing good grows from relationships built on intoxication.

Structure Is Still Love

Girls and boys thrive with:

- Boundaries
- Curfews
- Rules
- Check-ins

A curfew is not punishment.
It is a guardrail.

Knowing where a child is, who they are with,
and when they are coming home
is not control.
It is care.

Freedom without guidance is not freedom.
It is exposure.

Conversation Builds Connection

Ask your children:

- "What does safety mean to you?"
- "What kind of people do you feel comfortable around?"
- "How do you know when something feels wrong?"
- "What would you do if you ever felt unsafe?"

Do not only correct — communicate.
Connection gives parents influence.
Influence gives direction.
And direction builds protection.

Teach Boys, Too

A home that teaches safety to daughters must also teach respect to sons.

Teach them that:

- A woman's "no" is final.
- Alcohol is not an excuse for aggression.
- Power is not dominance.
- Masculinity is not violence.
- Real men protect, they don't prey.

We cannot protect girls while raising boys who become the danger.

What a Protective Home Looks Like

- A parent who answers the phone at any hour.
- A child who knows they can call for help without being shouted at.
- A parent who fetches when needed — not lectures when late.

- A family that talks openly about relationships, parties, and alcohol.
- A home where discipline and compassion walk hand in hand.

Safety grows in:

- Presence
- Patience
- Listening
- Example

Children copy what they see,
not only what they are told.

Final Reflection

A home that teaches and protects is not one that locks its doors —
it is one that opens conversations.

It is a home that says:

"You can always come to me."
"You are never alone."
"Your life matters more than your mistakes."

That kind of love
builds confidence,
teaches discipline,
and keeps our daughters and sons alive.

Chapter 10
Sisterhood, Mentorship & Watchfulness

There is a kind of love that does not come from blood —
the love of sisterhood.

It is the bond that says,

"I will not leave you behind."
"I will speak when you are silent."
"I will walk with you — not in front, not behind, but beside you."

In a world that can be unkind to women,
sisterhood is no longer a luxury.
It is protection.

The Power of Watchfulness

When we watch over one another, we do not gossip —
we guard.

Watchfulness is not about control;
it is about care.

It says:

- "Message me when you get home."
- "I'll wait until you're in the house."
- "You've had enough, let's go."
- "This guy doesn't feel right, let's leave."

Real friendship is not just taking photos together. It is protecting each other's safety, peace, and dignity.

Sisterhood is not proven by matching outfits — it is proven by who makes sure you come home alive.

When One Sister Falls Silent

Many tragedies begin with a girl who was too afraid to speak.
Afraid of judgment.
Afraid of being called "dramatic."
Afraid of being told, "You should have known better."

We must change that.

A true sister does not say:

"Why did you go there?"

She says:

"Are you okay?"
"You can tell me anything."
"Let's get help."

A safe sister listens without gossip.
She believes without conditions.
She helps without shame.

Because healing starts with being heard.

Mentorship — Passing Down Wisdom

In every generation, there are women who have been there —
who know what danger looks like,
who have made mistakes and survived them,
who carry lessons that could save another girl's life.

We need those women to speak.

Mentorship is not about perfection —
it is about passing down survival.

A mentor says:

"This is what I wish someone had told me."
"Here's what danger looks like before it happens."
"Here's how to leave quietly and safely."
"Here's how to rebuild yourself after pain."

When older women guide younger ones,
they turn pain into protection.

What Healthy Sisterhood Looks Like

1. We Check Each Other's Choices with Care
2. Not to criticize, but to make sure the decision is wise.
3. Ask: "Are you sure this is safe?" or "Do you have a plan to get home?"

1. We Set Group Standards for Going Out
   - No one leaves alone.
   - Everyone's phone stays charged.
   - We track each other's rides.
   - We make sure the one who drinks less stays most alert.
2.
3. We Warn Each Other About Dangers
   - "I heard this venue isn't safe."
   - "That guy has a bad reputation."
   - "She said she felt uncomfortable around him."
4.
5. That is not gossip — it's care.
6. We Protect Each Other's Names
7. We do not laugh when a friend makes a mistake.
8. We help her stand again.
9. Because shaming a girl for falling
10. will not keep the next girl from falling too.
11. We Celebrate Each Other's Growth
12. When one heals, we all heal.
13. When one succeeds, we all win.
14. When one learns, she teaches the rest.

That is the real "soft life."
A life softened by safety, support, and sisterhood.

How Men Benefit from Strong Sisterhood

Sisterhood does not exclude men — it educates them.

When women are united:

- Men are held accountable.
- Respect becomes expected.
- Abuse becomes harder to hide.
- Safety becomes a shared standard.

Because when women are divided, the system of silence stays strong.

But when women are connected, protection becomes collective.

The New Kind of Sisterhood We Need

We are no longer living in a time where sisterhood means only "friendship."
It must now mean:

- Protection
- Prayer
- Partnership
- Accountability

We must raise a generation of women who say:

"We don't compete — we cover each other."
"We don't laugh at mistakes — we learn from them."
"We don't just share makeup — we share wisdom."

Because one woman's safety
is every woman's safety.

Final Reflection

Sisterhood is how we rebuild the village again — one friendship, one circle, one shared conversation at a time.

Let every woman say:

"I am my sister's keeper."
"If she goes missing, I will not stay silent."
"If she's in danger, I will not look away."

That is how we heal a nation —
not just with laws,
but with love that watches.

Chapter 11
Bringing Back The Village

There was a time when a child was raised by more than two parents.
When a girl belonged not just to a household, but to a community.

If you stumbled, your neighbor caught you.
If you went missing, the whole street looked for you.
If you disrespected an elder, word reached your mother before you arrived home.

That was the South Africa that many of us grew up in —
the village that raised us.
The village that has gone silent.

It is time to bring it back.

The Village Was Our Protection

The village was not only about proximity.
It was about shared responsibility.

When something happened to one child,
it was everyone's business.

If a girl was seen walking with an older man,
someone would question it.
If a boy spoke disrespectfully,
someone corrected him.
If parents struggled,
neighbors stepped in.

We did not have wealth,
but we had watchfulness.
We had accountability.
We had moral courage.

That was our social safety net.

Where the Village Began to Fade

We lost our village slowly —
not through poverty alone, but through disconnection.

- Pride replaced humility.
- People stopped accepting correction or advice.

- Fear replaced trust.
- Neighbors became strangers.
- Technology replaced conversation.
- We speak to each other through screens, not hearts.
- Pain replaced patience.
- Many are too wounded, too tired, or too busy to get involved.

And so, we live beside one another —
but not with one another.

Our communities became quiet.
Our watchfulness disappeared.
And in that silence, danger found room to grow.

Bringing Back the Spirit of Ubuntu

Ubuntu is not a word we should only say on public holidays.
It is a way of life.
It means:

"I am because we are."

To bring back the village,
we must live Ubuntu again.

That means:

- Caring without being asked.
- Helping without expecting credit.
- Correcting without cruelty.
- Listening without judgment.
- Protecting without hesitation.

We rebuild community when we see each other again.

Restoring Accountability

A real village has boundaries.

- Adults correct the young.
- The young respect the old.
- Men protect women, not prey on them.
- Parents teach values, not just survival.
- Leaders serve, not exploit.

We cannot heal as a nation
while pretending morality no longer matters.

We cannot raise safe daughters
in a culture that rewards recklessness.

We must rebuild a moral foundation —
where doing what's right matters again,
even when no one is watching.

———

The Role of Men in the New Village

When good men go silent,
bad men get louder.

We need fathers, brothers, and sons who:
- Speak up when women are in danger
- Correct their peers when they cross the line
- Set examples of discipline and integrity
- Understand that masculinity is protection, not domination

The village cannot return
if men do not return to their role as protectors
and guides.

Not because women are weak —
but because unity is strength.

The Role of Women in the New Village

Women have always been the heart of the home, but today, they are also the backbone of the nation.

We must continue to:

- Mentor young girls
- Guide them without judgment
- Teach them to trust their instincts
- Remind them that their worth is not negotiable
- Build networks of women who protect, not compete

When women unite,
communities heal faster.
Because where women lead,
life follows.

Practical Steps to Rebuild the Village

1. Start with Your Street.
2. Greet your neighbors again. Know their names.
3. Exchange numbers for emergencies.
4. Community Watch with Compassion.
5. Watch over children and report danger — not with gossip, but with care.
6. Churches, Schools, and Clubs Must Reclaim Their Purpose.
7. These are not only meeting places; they are moral classrooms.
8. Let them teach life, values, and safety again.
9. Create Mentorship Networks.
10. Each adult woman mentors at least one younger girl.
11. Each man mentors a younger boy.
12. One relationship can redirect a destiny.
13. Talk About What's Hard.
14. Abuse, addiction, broken families — we fix nothing by hiding it.
15. Talking heals.
16. Silence kills.

1. Lead by Example.
2. A child who sees honesty learns truth.
3. A child who sees accountability learns responsibility.
4. A child who sees love learns safety.

The Village Is Not Gone — It Is Waiting

The village is not dead.
It is waiting for us to remember it.
To live again as people who see each other,
protect each other,
and love beyond family lines.

A nation does not change through government alone.
It changes through homes,
streets,
and neighbors who still care enough to knock on the door.

Closing Reflection

We lost our way when we stopped watching.
We lost our daughters when we stopped listening.
We lost our peace when we stopped caring.

But we can bring it all back —
not by returning to the past,
but by reviving the values that made us safe in it.

Bringing back the village
means bringing back humanity.
And humanity is how South Africa will heal again.

Closing Reflection

After everything I have seen, heard, and written in these pages,
I realise that this book is not just about parties, choices, or danger.
It is about a nation that has forgotten its heartbeat —
a nation that once raised children with fear, respect, and love,
but now buries them far too soon.

We have spoken about parents, community, and sisterhood.
We have looked at the pain behind the headlines and the silence that follows.
And after all of it, one truth remains:
South Africa is crying.

But I still believe she can be healed.
And so, as I close this book, I leave you with my greatest hope —
my wish for the country I still love.

My Wish for South Africa

As I close this book, my heart is heavy but hopeful.
Heavy because of what our country has become —
hopeful because I still believe we can change.

I dream of a South Africa where every child, especially every girl, can walk freely without fear.
Where fun does not end in tragedy, and safety is not a privilege but a right.
Where life is valued again — in our streets, our schools, and our homes.

I wish to see a nation where laws protect with strength and fairness,
where justice is swift and true,
and where consequences match the crimes committed.

Because right now, too many people kill, rape, abuse, and destroy lives
without fear of real punishment.
They know the system will delay, protect, or forget.
And that is why South Africa bleeds.

It is my wish that our leaders — with courage and conscience —
reconsider the death penalty as a deterrent for the most brutal and unforgivable crimes.
Not as revenge,
but as justice for the innocent lives taken without mercy.
As a reminder that life is sacred,
and that taking one must have the gravest consequence.

I long for a South Africa where people think twice before they take a life,
where drinking and driving is no longer treated lightly,
where violence, corruption, and substance abuse are no longer daily news,
and where every citizen is held accountable.

I dream of parents who raise children with integrity —
who know that doing the right thing matters even when no one is watching.
Of communities that care again — where neighbours notice, intervene, and protect.
Of leaders who lead with courage, conscience, and compassion.

May we rebuild a South Africa where:
- Men are protectors, not predators.
- Women are respected, not reduced.
- Children are guided, not neglected.
- And families become the first fence of safety again.

We have lost too many daughters. Too many sons.
Too many dreams buried too soon.

My wish is that we rise again —
not through politics or promises,
but through purpose, values, and love.

Because a great nation is not measured by its wealth,
but by how it protects the most vulnerable.

And I believe, still,
that South Africa can be great again —
if only we remember who we are,
and have the courage to change what we have become.

— Thuli Marutle Leigh
Author of "The Party Culture That Kills"

About the Author

Thuli Marutle Leigh is a South African-born international ESL teacher, writer, and storyteller dedicated to empowering the next generation through education, values, and truth.
She has spent years teaching English to children around the world, using creativity, compassion, and storytelling to build character, confidence, and respect among young learners.

Her passion for social change inspired The Party Culture That Kills — a powerful and thought-provoking book addressing the rising culture of recklessness, moral decay, and violence among today's youth. Through this work, Thuli calls for a return to integrity, accountability, and community — and for a South Africa where every young person can grow up safe, guided, and full of hope.

She believes storytelling can heal, awaken, and rebuild what society has lost. Her work continues to reflect her deep faith in humanity and her unshakable belief that South Africa can rise again — one home, one heart, one choice at a time.

Independently Published by Thuli Marutle Leigh

www.ingramcontent.com/pod-product-compliance
Lightning Source LLC
Chambersburg PA
CBHW032058150426
43194CB00006B/569